Roll the Wheel

Roll the Wheel

THE ABUNDANT LIFE AND WISDOM OF MAE PHILLIPS

Phyllis M. EagleTree

Roll the Wheel!
Best Wishes,
Phyllis EagleTree

FORSIGHT

Louisville, Kentucky

ISBN 978-0-9795109-0-8

Library of Congress Control Number: 2007906131

Book design by Images, Julius Friedman and Carol Johnson
Printed by The Merrick Printing Co., Louisville, Kentucky

Manufactured in the United States of America

ForSight
2718 Field Avenue
Louisville, Kentucky 40206

To my son, Jeffrey Scott

Jeffrey, this book is for you—for your inspirational spirit.

Like Mae, you teach and inspire with your life.

CONTENTS

Several years ago I traveled with my mother to her homeland of Kentucky. I had been there before, but I had not seen deeply into it. It was a geography I had taken for granted. My own roots ran down into the earth of the Great Plains and the Southwest, and I did not feel at home elsewhere. But throughout the years of my childhood my mother spoke to me of Kentucky, and always with such love and longing that it assumed in my mind the proportion of myth, a landscape of the imagination.

My mother was born at Fairview, near the border between Todd and Christian counties. Fairview is the birthplace of Jefferson Davis, president of the Confederate States of America during the Civil War, and it stands on the Trail of Tears, the route of the forced removal of the Cherokees from the Great Smokies to Oklahoma Territory during Andrew Jackson's administration. My maternal great-great-grandfather, I. J. Galyen, married a Cherokee woman and so brought the Indian strain into the blood of my maternal forebears.

In my mother's company, and in preparation for writing *The Names*, an autobiographical narrative, I visited the plain of the Little River, where my grandfather grew tobacco. I drove past Costellow, where he was born, and I lingered in Smith Cemetery, near Chandler's Chapel, where I. J. Galyen and his daughter Nancy (my great-grandmother) are buried close together. In the presence of familial ghosts I beheld the Land—the woods and streams, the hills and the seams of limestone, the waters and the grasses. I listened to the original speech of Kentuckians. I saw villages and farms and country stores. I saw children playing and men driving mules in the fields. I saw tobacco barns smoking in the misty brakes. And as I looked into the dark foliage and upon the sunlit meadows, I saw something of myself in the making. I touched the ground and felt the grain of my own blood in it.

When Phyllis EagleTree came to me and told me of her intention to write about an old woman of the Appalachian Mountains, my interest was immediately excited. And then when she showed me the photographs that she had taken of Mae Phillips I was convinced once and for all that here was a very significant work in progress. Phyllis EagleTree is a remarkably talented and perceptive woman, one whose sympathy and dedication are profound. Herself a Kentuckian, she is intimately connected to her subject, indeed a kind of daughter to Ms. Phillips. No one, I think, could better serve her subject, could be a more astute or sensitive observer, a more worthy friend and biographer. She brings to this work an extraordinary intelligence and gift of expression. When you read her text and see her photographs, you realize that you are in the presence of a human equation that reflects something of the best that is in us. Phyllis EagleTree takes us into a world apart, a world that is unfamiliar to many of us, but nonetheless a world of our knowing, one in which the human condition is set forth in words and images of great clarity and simplicity and goodwill. The Appalachian Mountains lie diagonally across eastern Kentucky. Harlan County is a concentration of the geographical, political, and cultural elements which define this region. And "region" is a word of particular meaning here. Nowhere else in America is the character of regionalism more closely realized in the soil, the forests, the rivers, and above all in the people of this hard, beautiful, and singular landscape.

In certain respects, Appalachia is remote, obscure to those who reside outside of it. From the time of settlement its inhabitants have preferred to keep to themselves, it seems, to mold their generations according to the ancient strictures of tradition and place. They are in some wise inaccessible. And yet they are a people of pervasive goodwill and generosity. They cherish their own; they are faithful to each other, to the land, and to the absolute providence which has always shaped their circumstances. In terms of material goods, some are impoverished. In terms of education, they lag behind most other Americans. Their economic opportunities are limited, and governmental support is unreliable. Notwithstanding, they persist and indeed prevail in their spirit. They know who they are; their identity is as secure as that of any people on earth, I suspect, and in their daily lives they find purpose and meaning, as well as challenge and resistance. Among their greatest resources is the element of survival. In them it is a sacred trust, a principle and a rule, a very reason for being.

Someone has said that only in being supremely regional can one be truly universal. Mae Phillips is a nearly perfect example of this axiom. She is one with her immediate environment. She is as native to her world as is the mountain laurel or the dogwood. She is a woman of our time and of that world, indeed of all times and every place, a distinct figure in our midst. She lives among us, and we are the richer for it. She is the intelligence and spirit of the soil.

Mae

Mae Phillips was born on October 11, 1912, at Jacks Creek in Leslie County, Kentucky. Her maiden name was Shepherd. Mae was the eldest of ten, with four sisters and five brothers: Gussie, Georgie, Lucy (who died as an infant), Lueannie (who died when she was five years old), Sheldon, Donley, Lewis, John, and McKinley (who died when he was three years old). The day McKinley died, Mae stood in her front yard and watched as he was carried away. She looked across the yard and saw her mother leaning on a rock at the edge of the woods, weeping.

Mae was very close to her father. She said that she worked like a man beside him. He taught her many valuable skills that would serve her well later in life.

When Mae was twenty-two years old, she met and married a man named Ova Phillips, called Ovie. Together they had nine children—three daughters and six sons: Jean, Louanna, Betty, Matt, Ollie (who was a twin to Matt and died as an infant), Kermit, Dennis, Estle, and Hubert. Mae raised a total of ten children, because she raised two of her grandchildren: Rose and Jeannie. She said when she first married Ovie he was a pretty good man, but within a few years he had taken up with bad company. He began to stay away from home for weeks at a time, and later, he would be gone for months.

Finally the day came when Ovie appeared at the front gate with a woman he had brought to stay. Mae saw them coming and was ready. She stepped out on the front porch with her shotgun and announced to Ovie that if he or the woman walked through the gate, she would kill them. She meant every word of it. Ovie and the other woman turned and went up the hill. That same afternoon, Mae filed for a divorce.

Turning Ovie away at the gate was the major turning point in Mae's life. She had to become totally self-sufficient and raise the children by herself.

Not long after Ovie and his new woman left, the new woman caught him asleep on their couch and shot and killed him. Mae buried him. She set the headstone.

Mae suffered more losses. By the early 1990s, three of her children had died. One child, Ollie, died at only two weeks; Matt, her eldest son, died when he was fifty-four; Bett, her youngest daughter, died when she was thirty-seven. Mae said that losing her children had nearly killed her.

Mae had found Matt in his truck close to her house. It was wintertime, and snow was on the ground. Mae shook Matt to try and wake him up, but he would not rouse, and Mae realized that he was dead. She barely made it back to the house.

In the same year, Bett was involved in a fatal car accident. Matt, Bett, Mae's brother Lewis, and her father and mother all died within a year and a half. But alongside Mae's grief over these soul-wrenching losses was a deep appreciation for being alive on this earth. She said, "Life gets rough sometimes, but nevertheless, we have to 'roll the wheel' [We have to do what it takes to keep life going]."

In order to provide for her children and herself, Mae often worked from before daybreak to after midnight. She grew a large garden, raised and sold hogs, repaired furniture, and traded with neighbors. She also worked for Dr. Lewis, and his son, Dr. P. O. Lewis, Jr., of Harlan, for fifteen years, cleaning and cooking for their families and taking care of the younger Lewises' four children. Mae worked seven days a week.

A typical day for Mae went like this: She would rise before dawn in order to prepare breakfast for her children and get ready to go to work at the Lewises'. She would walk to the Lewises' and work all day for them—cooking, cleaning, doing the laundry, and taking care of the little children. At the end of the day, she would walk home, arriving after dark. Then she would cook supper for her children, afterward washing clothes for them to wear to school. (Neighbors say they saw her hanging clothes on her clothesline at midnight.) Sometime after arriving home, in the midst of this night work, she would gather slop from the neighbors and feed her hogs.

Working for the Lewises enabled her to receive Social Security, her source of income. In order to pay for her house, Mae raised and sold hogs. She said she had a cow that gave good milk and a pretty white horse that she loved.

Through the years Mae became known for growing the finest garden around. Pictures of her garden appeared in local newspapers. She planted by the "signs," and she knew them by heart. She learned them from the *Ladies Birthday Almanac* and from her parents' teachings.

The image of Mae in her garden is an enduring one. It is night. The moonlight shines on Mae as she stands surrounded by her garden. She is smiling. The plants move in the silver light as a gentle breeze carries the scent of the rich turned earth.

Mae teaches us how to grow a fine garden and how to make a good life.

I was born on September 5, 1951. (By the time I was born, Mae had been living for almost forty years.) I grew up in Kettle, Kentucky, in Cumberland County, near Dale Hollow Lake and the Cumberland River—a few counties to the west of where Mae was born and raised. As an only child, I spent much of my time in the woods by the water. I explored valleys and streams. I explored the mountains where the streams seemed to fall from the sky. I listened to the sounds of water. At school age, I went to a two-room schoolhouse where we had cakewalks and box suppers. I married young and gave birth to my son, Jeffrey, when I was twenty-one years old.

I married twice, and after my first marriage I moved to Louisville, Kentucky, went to school, and later worked as a commercial photographer for twelve years to make a living for myself and my son. In 1990, my last year working as a corporate advertising photographer, I moved to Chicago. My son was now grown and had joined the Navy. I was at a turning point in my life. I began to think about my life, about what I had done with myself and my time. I made a decision about what I wanted my next chapter to be: I wanted to be a channel for wisdom. I took a napkin out of a basket that was sitting on top of my desk, and I called the telephone number written on it.

The number I called was that of Jerry Johnson. He was a neighbor of Mae Phillips in Evarts, Kentucky, near Harlan, in Harlan County. He was in his forties, and Mae loved him like a son. Jerry was a coal miner who had gone on strike with other miners during the Brookside Mine strike in 1973. His back had been injured in three mine cave-ins. Six months earlier, I had traveled from Chicago to attend a preview of a documentary film about Appalachia, at the Kentucky Center for the Arts, in Louisville. Jerry had a role in the film and was present at the showing to answer questions. After the discussion, I met Jerry. We talked, and he suggested that I meet Mae. He said she had an unusually strong spirit and a very good heart and that she would have much to teach people about living. I thanked Jerry for telling me about Mae and took the napkin with their names on it back to Chicago.

During my phone conversation with Jerry six months later, we made arrangements so that I could come to Evarts, and he could take me to meet Mae Phillips, who was then seventy-nine.

On the day our first meeting took place, Jerry and I walked through Mae's gate, and she gave us both a welcoming hug. Jerry and Mae had not seen each other for quite some time, and they were happy to have a chance to visit. Part of the first chapter of this book, "The Meeting," comes from that first visit. I later moved into a small coal-camp house a couple of houses down from Mae's, and I lived there for a year and a half.

After a time of our visiting back and forth with one another, Mae, Jerry, and I would make a journey together back to the homeplace at Jacks Creek, in Leslie County, where Mae's mother and father had lived and where Mae had spent part of her time growing up. On this trip we would also visit the graveyard where Mae's husband, Ovie, was buried and where Mae had buried one of her children. The recording of this journey makes up the second chapter of this book, which is entitled "Traveling to the Homeplace." When Mae had last been at the homeplace, her mother and father had been alive. She said, "It's hard to look. This is a hard thing for me, and anybody knows just within reason how it is." I wanted to leave and take her with me, but I stayed and we walked through the rooms together. Later Jerry took us to the graveyard, and we walked around the stones marking some of Mae's family. It was hard to look. We came home.

Back on Mae's porch in Evarts, sitting on her green bench, Mae and I told each other many of the stories of our lives. We learned much about one another as the months passed. Her porch is a short distance away from the headwaters of the

Cumberland River. Clover Fork, one of the forks of the Cumberland, flows by her yard. I liked learning that our lives share a river.

The final chapter of this book, "Back on Mae's Porch," is made up of some of the conversations Mae and I had on the porch after we returned from our traveling.

Sitting on the front porch, I especially liked watching Mae's hands in the morning light. Mae has large, powerful hands. She once told me that she would go right on living as long as her hands would work.

I watched Mae go right on, and I listened to her stories. I saw how she lived, and I learned.

I learned that the foundation for a life like Mae's is reverence for life itself. I learned that in those times when life becomes such that we feel like dying, we must reach down inside ourselves and grab hold of our strength and will to affirm life— no matter what the circumstances. I learned that much meaning comes from this affirmation. This reverence for life may inform all of our choices. I saw, with Mae, that this foundation was the beginning of an abundant life. I saw that she recognized every life as important. She paid attention to the promptings of her heart and gave freely, whether this was encouragement, food from her garden, or a warm place so someone could come in out of the cold. I observed that Mae nourished not only human life but also animals, plants, every living form of life. All life is of "the wheel," and it is a privilege to be a part of this "rolling of the wheel."

I began to sense that the real valuables in life consist of exchanges between people. Mae created an intimate community filled with rich exchanges. During my first two weeks in my small house in Evarts, I became the recipient of a gift. I had been invited by my neighbors, Mary Johnson and her son Tim, to go to church. (Mary is the biological mother of Jerry Johnson, although he was largely raised by Mae.) Word got out that I did not have a dress or shoes to wear to church, and that I wanted to go. A few mornings later, I awoke to find a white plastic bag hanging on my door with a pink ribbon around it. Inside the bag was a pink dress—just my size. There was no note. That afternoon, as I walked back from seeing Mae, I noticed a row of high heels lined up near my doorstep, and beside them was Jerry Johnson. He had gone to some of the women in the community, and they had given him their high heels for me to wear to church. I tried on a pair that fit and smiled. I had received generosity and good wishes, one of the many rich exchanges that would take place in the community of Evarts.

I learned that when you express a generosity of spirit or are the recipient of such, you also receive yet another gift: You are enabled to feel the interconnectedness of all life. You get to feel a river of goodwill flowing between people. Joy arises from this river. This is experiencing life more abundantly. In this community, where Mae's house sits on the side of a mountain, people know one another's stories. They know each other's troubles, and they know each other's personal celebrations. In this knowing of one another's needs, they know when to appear and generally what to say and give when they arrive. It is a free-flowing river.

This river has honor in its currents—the honor of a person's name and all that name comes to mean, the honor in being able and willing to help your neighbors and family, the honor of making your word good, doing what you said you would. This is the quality of being there for another. Beyond this, a person's name stands with a determined measure of integrity representing honesty, responsibility, and good-heartedness. Mae told me about going around paying off Ovie's debts after he had died. The store owners told her she did not have to do this. She replied, "But my children live under the name of Phillips." I learned that these exchanges you have with yourself, and the exchanges you have with others, can lead to feelings of deep satisfaction and contentment.

Contentment comes into your being when you are satisfied with what you are being about. This is the heart's celebration. And Mae shows us that this state of being gives rise to good humor. She has a ready smile. She tells stories of funny happenings and celebrative stories of music, dancing, and singing. Her family is known as the "songbirds of the mountains."

Mae's stories of loss mingle with her stories of thankfulness and humor. She shows there can be celebration even in the midst of grieving. Embracing the whole experience of being alive, she "rolls the wheel" and lives a life rich in meaning and fulfillment. She brought nine children into being and raised ten. A great sustainer and celebrant of life, she instructs us, too, to roll the wheel.

THE MEETING

Dennis was a baby when we come here. I've got a record of it in my Bible. They've all got birth certificates and Social Security numbers. There's a lot of people lets their children get grown and ain't got a birth certificate. I was over forty years old when I made my birth certificate. I went over in Leslie County where I was raised and born, and them people that was there when I was a young baby was there to sign my birth certificate.

Yeah, and they're all dead now. All of them is dead and gone. I was forty years old, but I swear it's so strange for me to be till I can't just climb on top of the house—and could if I was really to set my head to it yet. It's just not me a-wanting to. And I just take care and multiply and lay back. When anyone can't help theirself, I just give them anything they need that I've got.

I don't need for nothing. But I can live on a flat rock, honey. You know, they's so much waste. They's enough throwed away and wasted up and down here for anything. And it's wrong to throw things away.

We've got a good world to live in and to appreciate that God give us. And we can go to a resting place sometime. But I ain't got a thing between me and God, and I ain't been mean to nobody.

That child Jerry come here, and him little. I've got up—and it way in the night and a snow on the ground—and opened the door, and he's went in here and slept with us. God knows everything, and everything that ain't right is wrong. But God knows my heart. And I'm crazy about children and people that's older than I am. And I can't feel like I'm old to save my life without I look in the glass.

LIVING'S WORTHWHILE

Being old is creeping up on me. See, I'm seventy-nine years old. All through my life I ain't never missed making a garden. My garden washed off the hill last year, and I've got canned stuff all over the place. I dug my tater patch. I kept the awfulest hole of taters holed up in the garden, and I took them up this spring. And you ought to see'd them taters. I had fifty pounds of taters, and after Matt died, I just didn't have no use for them.

Matt would come and ask me, "You wouldn't happen to have beans cooked? Some pinto beans and buttermilk?" And he'd laugh. But I was always prepared when he'd come to the house to have what he wanted to eat.

You know God loves a cheerful giver. It makes me feel good down in my heart to give anyone anything, or feed them.

But I'm telling you now, living's worthwhile.

OVIE WAS GONE

The children was just baby-like. They was just one little-un
and then another little-un. They wasn't no one to help me. Ovie
was gone. He'd leave, and he'd go off and stay two and three
weeks at a time. But I had a hog—a hog that was in good shape.
It got cold weather, and I gathered all of the corn off of the field
and fed the hog, and then I didn't have no more feed, ner no
money, but the hog was fat. And me and Lewis, my brother,
we killed that hog.

Why, I'd shoot a hog between the eyes and scald it and bleed
it like Papa was right with me. I worked right by the side of my
daddy at anything that would come along.

Oh, I've done everything to try to raise my children and
to keep something to eat. Now I've got food in every corner.
You won't starve to death here.

I sent them children to school every one of them—took
them to church. Them two grandchildren I raised, them two girls.
That made me ten children.

THE STROKE

See, I had that stroke. I was in the Lexington Hospital five months. I didn't know one person from another, and I didn't know my children. I stayed over at Gussie's a month and didn't know where my house was.

It was known all over for a week here that I was dead, but they sure got a fooling. And I come right back and stood on a walker out there on the road and made them plant my taters. I sure did. If I can't get along one way, I'll try another.

HUNTING THE SHADE SPOTS

Matt was a young baby. I packed a washtub to set him in with a quilt doubled four-square, and I put that quilt in there till he couldn't bump himself against the tub. And then I opened the umbrella and stood it up over him. I'd hoe corn from one place to another. I'd just hunt the shade spots. I packed him with me, and then I'd hoe, and then I'd feed him. And if he got sleepy he could lay down.

Miss Johnson went on vacation, and I gave her a twenty-dollar bill just to be a-giving it to her. Yeah. And when Matt was dead, she brought flowers, and she brought money here. She brought the money so if it was needed worser for food or something or other. God bless her.

People needs just to be good and treat one another right, and keep the wheel a-turning. If it goes to stopping, help roll the wheel. Yeah. And when Miss Johnson and Tim went on vacation, I gave Miss Johnson twenty dollars so she could buy her some little things to make herself feel good. We're just like children—me and Miss Johnson. We've been together since Matt died.

THE RED WAGON

I went on the mountain and dug flower trees—dogwoods and papaws. I've got a papaw tree full of papaws out there by my coal pile. And I've got the awfulest lot of coal under the floor that you've ever seen. I've got five, six, or eight tons of coal under the floor. See, the sun can't get to it, and the sun can't draw the oil out of it.

I have a little old red wagon out there. Faye Coffee gave me a little old bitty wagon, and it was bent all to pieces. I brought it up here, beat it out, and cleaned it up. And oh, it tickled the young-uns to death—that little worn-out wagon a-sitting up there at the end of the porch. They said it's just so much like my daddy's things that's down home.

But I got in an awful bad shape. I got till I couldn't do nary a thing with my hands with that arthritis. Well, I'd take that little wagon down there and would lay me some blocks of coal in it. With the weight of me I could pull the coal up the hill with the wagon, but I couldn't pack a bucket in my hand. The weight of the bucket a-pulling down on me hurt me, but that little wagon would roll. I've had to bring one block of coal in at a time to put in that stove 'cause I couldn't pack nothing, sure have, but I did. I put it in anyhow. I'd just pull my red wagon.

SIX YEARS OLD AND SICK

I swear I've tried to live good since I was six years old. When I was six years old, I was sick one time, and I told Mammy to put me something down till I could lay on the floor. Oh, I was so sick. I was just trying to find somewhere to rest. And there was an old man that came down the road. He went to church and preached. I said to Mammy, "Mammy, when Joe comes down tell him to come by." I said, "I want him to pray and lay his hands on me." And he did. And Joe never more than got on down the road till I was up off that pallet and feeling better and playing.

BROTHER SHEL

My oldest brother, Shel, told somebody, "I wish you'd had
my sister with you a little while. She'd have showed you what side
to put the butter on." Yeah. When Mammy would get gone, Shel
would try to fight the children. He'd go to throwing rocks in the
house. And I'd just run right through the rocks and get ahold of
him and wear him out. And when Mammy and Papa would come
home, Shel would kind of tell that I had whupped him. I'd just
tell them what it was for. Pap would say, "Why, just give him
another if he goes to a-bothering them little children." I can't
stand for a bigger young-un to run over a baby.

One time Pap sent me and my brother to look for his mules. Those mules had gone to Jessie Fork over in Leslie County. Pap had a mule named Bill, and Pap wanted that mule. We looked for them mules, but we couldn't find them. So we hit that mule sign, and just kept following the sign. We just kept going. We went about three miles up the creek. Me and ole Shel went right up that holler after them mules. And we was going up that fork, and we saw a man a-catching ole Bill to put a bridle on him. He had a harness and a bridle. And we had our bridle on our arm to get one of them mules. And we went up there, and I hated to call on that man so bad, but I said, "Buddy, that's our mule, and me and my brother's after him, and would you mind us a-getting him?"

And he said, "Well, I was going to plow a little in my garden with both of them."

Well, I said, "I'm sure sorry that we come at this time. I wouldn't, and my daddy wouldn't, have cared a bit for you to plow the mules." Well, one mule didn't have no bridle, but we had one bridle, and I put that bridle on him. That mule was named Sam. He was cross-eyed.

Well, I went over there on that hill to a hickory tree. I packed a big knife all the time when I was out in the woods. You know you can start skinning a hickory at the bottom and pull the bark up, and it'll skin plumb out. It's just a width like. I cut that bark and pulled it up. That man didn't know what to think, but that's what my daddy taught me, you see. Well, I got that bark that's tender and that would tie good. You know that they's holding teeth in a mules's mouth. They's a place right across here that they ain't no teeth, and two big teeth are there. I put that bark behind them holding teeth and tied it in a knot under there. I got on that mule, ole Bill, and run him ever jump to Jacks Creek where my daddy's house was. We went up Brush Fork and over across the mountain. We went down in the back of our field and hit home. We knowed every clear cut around the tops of them mountains and down in the woods. We could go anywhere.

RIDING ROAN IN THE NIGHT

One time we had an old cow named Roan, and we went to Jones Creek, and it was nearly plumb black dark—me and my oldest brother. We went over there and got ole Roan. Roan had a bell on. I put ole Shel on that cow, and I got on, too. I put Shel in front so I could hold him. And I just reached back there and got that cow's tail till we couldn't slide over her head. And old Roan just walked with us, and that bell was a-knocking, till she packed us right into the barnyard at Pap's.

We done that to keep from getting snakebit. We was out in the black dark, in the green weeds, and was afraid of getting snakebit. And that old cow, well, we could just ride her to the house just like riding a mule. I held the cow by the tail and held Shel with my other hand. And Shel held to the bell collar, and we come right over across Jones Creek Hill that way. And Pap didn't know, and the stars was shining, and the moon was up as we went around the hill there at home. We was just little young-uns.

CARRY ME CAREFUL

One time Pap went off and got drunk, and he stayed late, and Mammy was worried about him, and she told me to go down the road and see where he was. And blessed God, he had fell off of his mule. Pap was drunk, and his foot was hung in the saddle stirrup. And that mule was a-dragging him. And they was mud holes up that road—soft mud. And Pap would say, "Boys, carry me careful." And that mule was a-dragging him. He thought there was someone a-packing him, he was so drunk. And Lord, I caught that mule easy and calm. I unbuckled the saddle and let the saddle down to get the stirrup down to get Pap away from that mule.

We made a living on our farm. And we raised everything that we ate. We had plenty of food.

I bet you all had fun too.

We did. We did. And when we broke to go to the house, them boys would get their banjo and guitar, and Pap would get the songbook. And we'd all go to singing and would eat supper and have the best time, and before we went to bed we'd just have the biggest good time, after working all day.

It never hurt us to work. Mammy would have a big supper cooked, and we'd eat hearty and have our cows milked and put away. And them boys would fall into that music, and we'd have music way into the night. And it was just us—just the family a-having the finest time ever was. And Pap would be a-swinging us around, and he'd be a-dancing with us. Bless his old heart. Anyone could come, and he would be so happy over them a-coming to see us. He'd jump out in the yard and dance all over the place. Yeah he would. He'd be so tickled over them a-coming.

Pap made a good time. People would come to our house just to talk to him and to be with him 'cause he would joke. He would laugh and talk to them. And it was a good pastime.

People's too mean about it now to do anything. If they get together, they go a-wanting to fight or something or other. But that's because, well, it's just a time.

SWAPPING A DOG TO A GUITAR

My brother Lewis started playing music when he was a baby. Why, when he was a-sitting in the floor, he couldn't walk yet, but he knowed when a banjo or a guitar was tuned up. He'd make Mammy turn the screws till it sounded right. And he couldn't pick the banjo up. It was laying across his lap, but he would take his thumb and thumb every one of the strings to see if they sounded right. And he'd make Mammy keep turning till it did. And honey, he started off right there playing right in the floor. And I went and swapped a dog to a guitar for him.

I went across the mountain, and I traded a woman a dog to a guitar she had—a good guitar. Yeah. And I come walking right back in with it. He was talking over that just before he died, Lewis was. And I've got his picture with that guitar that I bought for him with a dog. Him and Matt was about that high with their coveralls on. They were the sweetest things that you ever seen.

NAVY BLUE

I've got good shoes and good clothes. I can't hardly get out from under a job long enough to put me on some good clothes. Well, I fixed up to go to Leslie County 'cause Chester Sizemore died. He was a neighbor of ours, and he used to give us work to do. Me and Pap and my brother would work for Chester. We hoed his big field of corn for twenty-five dollars.

Yeah, I fixed up to go to Leslie County. Oh, I want to dress up when I start back home where I was raised. I put on my navy blue then. And I went to Miss Johnson's, and Tim said, "Well, I liked to not have known Ms. Phillips." Said, "What about Ms. Phillips? Did you see her dressed up this morning?"

Miss Johnson said, "Ms. Phillips is a good-looking woman when she dresses up and wants to go out and see her people."

It was summertime, and I was barefooted and me a grown woman. I was going to work in the fields through the week, and then when I'd come home, I'd clean up. My aunt Dixon that's dead, the sister to my mammy, she about give me what clothes that I had a-growing up. She had girls, and when they would outgrow the really good old clothes, why, she'd give them to me.

SHEEP SHEARING

We had our sheep and sheared the sheep. And me and Mammy and my daddy, we would wash that wool. Me, a little girl, I would go over there and pick the burrs out of the wool, and wash that wool, and get it in shape to send to Rosenbaum—off to a factory. And we would have clothing made, or we could get the money for the wool, or have cloth. Mammy always sent and had stuff to make suits out of that sheep wool. It was made in suit cloth till you could make suits, skirts, and jackets for women.

And I would hold the sheep's feet crossed till they wouldn't be a-kicking Mammy and her a-shearing.

BOLSTER PILLOWS

We'd pick our geese and take the feathers and sell the feathers for three dollars a pound. And ducks, I've got duck feather pillows and a feather bed that come off of them ducks down home when I was a little girl. I wouldn't take nothing for it. Talking about resting good at night.

They's feathers to pick off of the geese. You can get above their hip here where the long feathers is. Them's called bolster feathers. Mammy'd pick these. She'd say she wanted to get them bolster feathers good. She'd put them in her pillow. I've got a long pillow plumb across the head of my bed. I made it. One end of the pillow's got feathers from some ducks that Ovie killed on the water down here. I saved them feathers off of them ducks that he killed—wild ducks. We had that pillow on our bed.

CHRISTMASTIME

We never had nothing. We never had a Christmas tree, and I won't have one 'cause we never had nary one and us little. It's a fine holiday, and I put in every way I can to sponsor it, but it gets to me too much. It sure does.

But now I've got two dolls that cost three hundred dollars. I named one after that teacher astronaut. That doll's hair is black and hangs down her back, and she has a green velvet dress on. She has a hat on and a handbag on her arm and button shoes on.

Well, as I say, Mammy'd fry sausage and make sweet bread, and she would try to make things for us. She popped corn balls and done everything. We done everything that we could do. We just didn't have a big lot of money, but we had plenty of food.

We couldn't buy no little cute things nor didn't have no presents, but me and ole Shel would saw some blocks and get a big log and make a hole in it and make us a wagon. We'd get up on the hill with it, and we would slide off of that hillside— the wheels just a-flying. We had a good time. And we'd dig a big hole back in the ground, and then we'd set a door shutter over the face of it. We could just walk back in that bank and stand up. We was back there in the cave. We'd dig. We'd dig all week a-getting a hole dug for a hideout.

THE CAVE AND THE CAT

We had a cave at home that had rooms, and it was just like a-going in a house. Yeah. And when it would snow, we would get fresh eggs at the house and use a kettle and water and go up there to the cave and build us a fire. It was set up just like a house. And we would boil eggs and eat and have lunch out in that snow up there under that cliff. And that ivy would be a-hanging over the edge. We'd have mountain tea with red berries. And oh, we took off to the cave every time that it snowed. Why, we had the best time in that mountainside.

And I had an old cat. Dice Doris give her to me. That woman was named Dice. Well, the cat had kittens and was gone a long time, and I thought she was killed. There was a hollow log above the house, above our garden, and I went up there to get Mammy some stove wood and pick up little sticks for kindling.

Well, my cat was up there with a gang of kittens, and them kittens were all sitting out on a log. Talking about something pretty was that cat and that gang of kittens. She had them in that log, and they'd come out in the sun sitting there, just rolled up together—like a picture in a book. And I thought so much of that old cat. And that cat would go to the cave with us and take her kittens with her.

GIVING OUT THE EGGS

Mammy would go and get an apron full of eggs. They had fresh eggs all over the place in boxes. Pap would get on his mule and hand them eggs out to people down the creek. He'd take bucketfuls and give to 'em.

Pap had three hundred chickens. He had three hundred chickens of all sizes. Oh God, there were chickens all over the place.

God, we'll never forget the things that's been—what's gone by.

LITTLE TOY WRISTWATCH

Honey, I just worked on things. When I went to school,
I tried to be just like my teacher. I had a little old toy wristwatch
with a little old black band on it. It wasn't nothing. And I put it
on, and I felt like I was worth a million dollars, all dressed up.
She was a woman teacher, and I set right close pretty much to
where she was. And oh, I'd just study my book, with my watch
on my arm, like I was as grown as I am today. I enjoyed myself,
but I thought she was the prettiest thing, and I tried to be just
like her. I always tried to copy after good things. And I am so
proud. Reckon what caused me to do it?

THE FIGHT

I practically went to the sixth grade. Yeah. And could read, Lord. Why, they had a stack of them little books for little children, and I'd read through every one of them. But you know what I would have liked to have been—I would have liked to have got to go to school and been a teacher.

And me and a girl got to fighting, and ole Shel caused us to get into a fight. That girl come down there and walked right up on my feet, and I said, "What are you doing?"

She said, "Why, you old Matt Shepherd-looking thing." Honey, calling me after my daddy. And I thought the sky had fell because she said that about my daddy. Honey, I knocked her down and choked her. She had an old cap on, and it just come down over her mouth. She had a habit of biting people. I just knocked that cap right down over her face and grabbed her right under the neck. I scooted her through that mud. They was mud all over her. And when she got up, I grabbed at a stump, and God knows I didn't know what I was a-grabbing—just anything to kill her with. And that stump, blessed goodness, just pulled out of the ground. It just jerked up when I wanted it. And I cracked her right over the head and shoulders with that stump. She hit that Beech Mountain a-running like a turkey, and the next morning when she came back to school, Mr. Diedrick told us to stay in.

He said, "You-uns go on out. I want to talk to Mae." He wouldn't keep me in. He said, "Mae, you stay five minutes, and then go right on out." And he said, "What did you-uns fight over?"

I said, "She walked on my feet and called me after my daddy. And I don't want no one a-talking to me about my daddy."

"Well," he said, "you stay in five minutes, and give them time to get out, and then you go on out." He never held me in. Next morning here she come. I said, "Don't you come and get in the seat with me." I didn't want her to sit with me.

And one time she bit me. We went down to their house, and she bit me on the arm, and then Mammy knocked the pure fire out of her right in front of her mother, Mammy did. Mammy'd shoot a gun or anything. She just knocked that girl. When Mammy seen the print of her mouth on my arm, Mammy knocked her like a-hitting a fence post. Mammy said to her mother, "Come here, and look at what that girl done to Mae's arm." Well, that woman never said nothing much. Mammy said, "She'd sure better stay a-loose from Mae's arm a-biting." Said, "I'll have her killed and not know it." Oh God, I'm a-telling you what's the God's truth.

Well, when we was a-fighting at school—when the morning come, right here she come with a stick to sit by me. And I said,

"I want you to get out of here." And I said, "Mr. Diedrick, I don't want her sitting with me." I said, "Now she caused me to get in trouble yesterday." And I said, "It'll be again today." I allowed she'd be a-wanting to fight, but I'd have worn her out again.

And she said, "I want to sit with little Mae." She acted like she loved me real good. But then she beat Nell Mattford up every day. She'd bite Nell, have her black and blue all over. But honey, I choked her till her tongue lolled out. And them children was rattling the dinner buckets and refereeing over me a-whupping her. She whupped everything she come to, but she never whupped me.

And I whupped ole Shel good for a-running off and not a-helping me. He helped start it, and then he run off, and when I got him, I give him some of it. He laughs his head off over it right now. Oh, we had a good time.

2 TRAVELING TO THE HOMEPLACE

See, I ain't been over here in so long. It seems everything has growed up worser, and it looks so strange. We'll have to cross the mountain to go down Jacks Creek. Now right there's the Essie post office. We're on the right road. I used to come this way a-walking, and I would be so tired.

I used to work at home in the summer and then go in the winter and work at Hyden. I stayed with my aunt and helped her cook for workhands, and I'd buy Mammy everything and bring it home to her, get her new sheets, and brooms, tablecloths, and new dishes. I was twenty years old then.

Yeah. I went to living on my own when I was about twelve years old, raised me a garden at the house every year. I had a garden and me just a young-un. I growed tobacco. I tried to act like Aunt Jane Naper that lived right over here. She would put little rocks around her tobacco plants, and then she would lay a paper over the plants. She'd put the rocks on the paper to hold it down. She did this to keep the sun from killing out the plants. When I'd set my tobacco out, I'd put the paper like Aunt Jane did. Yeah, I was a-copying after her. I just had a few little tiny rows of tobacco, but to make me have a garden like Aunt Jane's, I'd have cucumbers and everything.

I'd study they's an old frame of a stove that was rolled up in a holler. It was above where our old house was up the creek where I was raised. I'd study how could I get that old frame of a stove and get me a house started. Oh, I'd be a-laying in the bed, and I was a-lifting in my mind, getting that stove so I could make me a house. I was determined to get me a house to live in somewhere.

I've been pretty lucky over it. I ain't had everything, but we fared good and had something to eat, and could sleep good, could sit down, and ain't done without too much.

They was a lot that we could have enjoyed that we didn't have time to, but we could work and be together and enjoy ourself. We'd be so happy. Mammy was a-cooking good meals, and we'd be coming out of the field to eat dinner. We'd lay down and sleep awhile after we'd eat, and then we would get up and go again—the cool of the evening a-being a-coming. We'd hoe a big lot. Me and my ole brother could hoe corn as fast as Pap could plow it with a mule. Pap just about hoed the corn with his plow and mule.

THE DOG ROCK

It wasn't like this when I lived here. It wasn't growed up. It's 'cause we ain't used to nothing but good highways and everything. When you come back into this neck of the woods, honey, it ain't like being out where everything is going on. A many a step I've made up and down here going to school.

Me, and another little girl, and a little boy, we had to pack our dinners in buckets. We would sit down and divide our dinners. We'd swap out and have a good dinner.

Right up here's a rock where I hit a dog with a rock. That dog was trying to bite me, and it had its mouth open, and I hit right in the middle of its mouth with a rock. I was trying to get on the mule behind my daddy. Pap said, "That dog's gonna bite you." And about that time, that dog opened its mouth big. I throwed that rock, and it hung right in the locks of the dog's jaw. There, that's the rock right there, the rock that I got on to get up on Pap's mule. I swear it's a wilderness, but it comes natural.

FLOWERS WHILE I LIVE

I wasn't here much after I was about twenty years old. When you get a family you can't visit much, nor go on vacations, nor nothing. When you've got a family, you've got something to keep you busy, to can, cook, wash, and everything.

I ain't had nobody to back me up in nothing. If I'd had, I'd had a fortune. Why I've give people stuff, and right now I don't need a thing. I enjoy having things, and if anyone loves me good enough to want to give me some little thing, why, I appreciate it so much it's a sight.

Jerry, thank you so much for these beautiful flowers.

You know now he's giving me flowers while I live, and when I'm gone he won't forget it.

A TIME CLOCK

We're like a time clock. We've got somebody that keeps the time, and if they don't help us along, we won't run. We'll quit. It's the truth.

But you know, now they's rough things to live through, and we've got a rough road to travel to meet the Lord. I know the Lord will move right in your mind when anything's wrong and will tell you not to do it. He sure will. They's things comes to me just like someone a-coming and telling me. When I feel worried, I can't talk to anyone, and I ain't happy. They'll be something a-going on, and you'll hear of it in just a little while. That's the way it works out every time. Oh God, when I heard Bett, I said to them, "Do you reckon Bett's killed?" They told me it was true. But now what hurt me too was going out there and finding Matt dead in that truck. That just knocked me plumb out. It did. I never sat down till I got every dollar paid on his burial and his marker, and I miss him more every day.

CANNING TOMATOES AND BETT DEAD

I want to get good tomatoes that's good to eat right at the time. They're the kind that you can with and make your tomato juice with. I've got a box of quart cans—a whole case of tomato juice that I've made. And it's the best stuff ever was. And I'm so busy, I can't get time to hardly go and hunt it and get it.

I canned tomatoes when Bett was dead, me and John. Little John stayed with me. My tomatoes had come in, and they was a-laying and rotting. And I canned tomatoes and her dead. Bett was dead. I was here with that baby and them all gone but just me and little John. And I couldn't do nothing else. And I just went and picked the tomatoes and canned and saved them, so I could give them to those that came back—not let the tomatoes rot up after we raised them. Wouldn't have been no sense in that.

BETT

I can't help but think that you're made just like Bett, and you act just like Bett. And Bett was head-on to do her own thing. And she could do anything she took ahold of. She could splice belts in the mines. She could do any kind of mechanic work and electrical work. She went to the electricians' school, and she made a hundred on everything she studied on.

Oh, you would have been tickled to death to have gotten to see her and be with her. She was a fine person, and she was so cute. She put on her coveralls with galluses and a red handkerchief around her neck. She wore her bank cap, and her battery was on her hip, and her light was on her head. And honey, she'd take her hair around like that and put it up under her cap, and that just made it look like her hair was short. And I swear she was the prettiest thing in that mining outfit—that was so much like her daddy that I thought it'd kill me. Her shoes, her dipped-up shoes that she worked in, looked just like his shoes. Lord have mercy, them shoes is in the house somewhere.

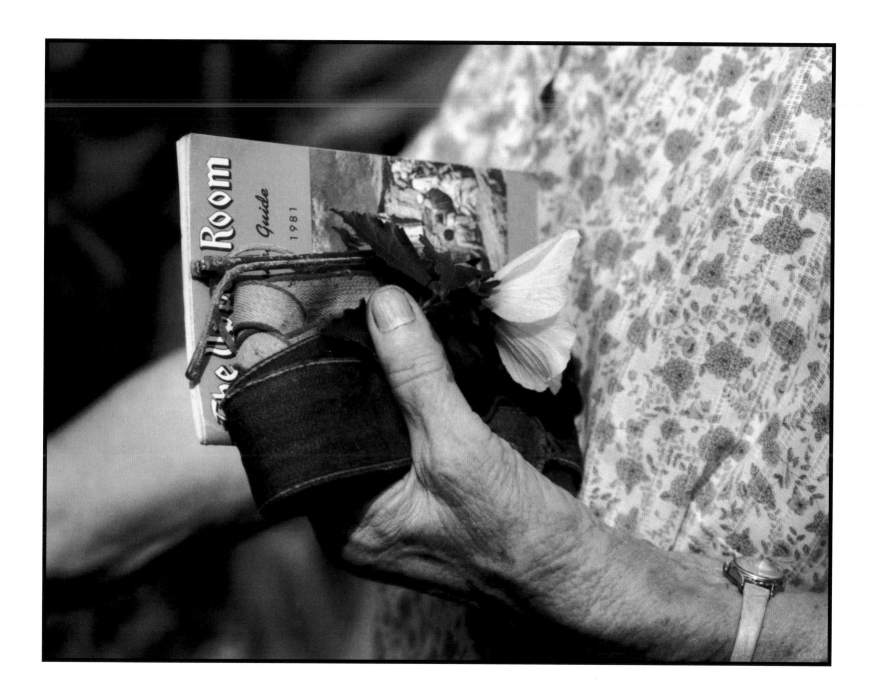

PUTTING A STONE TO A GRAVE

This is a pretty place. Yeah. What about all of the money people spends, and they'll just let their people's graves go. Buddy, I believe in putting a stone to a grave and the date of their birth. That's all they've got. Just as soon as one of mine dies, they's a rock goes to its head. And it ain't a piece of one either. I'd plumb forgot how Ovie's tombstone was. I thought it was more of a pale blue. But it's a good rock. And blessed goodness, I had to bring it up here.

There was a fight started every time that tombstone was named to bring. At the house those young-uns would get to disagreeing. I finally went and got Elmer Couch's truck, and me and Hubert and Joyce just brought it on.

Them children wanted to fight one another when they'd go to do anything about setting that headrock up. I don't know why. I guess they was hurt over their daddy and then just wanted to take it out on one another. I just had to go ahead and live and do what I could. I couldn't have them to do nothing. They'd just get in a fight with one another, wanting to be mean, and I couldn't fool with them. But they'll be a brighter day somewhere. Yeah. The sun will shine.

WORKING ON THE GRAVES

And what about Ovie got up and went off and picked up the sorriest old woman ever was and left us. And I had to send them children to school and do the best that I could. But Ovie's been dead and pushing up daisies so long.

I've never been with another man since. I've never seen nothing that's entertained me. It's not in my heart. I just couldn't do it.

You know what, that man that I married, that was my children's daddy, he was the man, and when he went away like he did, that just took ever bit of confidence that I had. He took the sorriest human that was up this hollow and left me and my children. He just walked down in the mud and left us to live or die.

And that woman caught him asleep and shot his brains out. And then when he had to be buried, they came to get me to bury him.

I put a tombstone to his grave. I went down there and put that tombstone up myself. Hubert backed the truck right up to Ovie's grave, and we scooted it off. I took my new mattock with me, and a jar of water, and cement, to cement that headrock down in that foundation rock. And I dug the pit out and put that foundation rock in with my mattock—laid that rock down, and set it right the way I wanted it. Ovie's got as pretty a grave that's on that hill.

I wouldn't sit down till there was a marker laid across Matt's grave either. I give four hundred fifty dollars for that marker that's on Matt's grave. I wouldn't let a crack be—I wouldn't let that water go down in around him. No sir. I went and filled his grave up with fine railroad rocks and got that rich dirt and filled them cracks up.

BURIED ON MY BIRTHDAY

That bullet's a-laying right in Ovie's chest in that grave that that woman put him in. Ovie got himself killed. And he left us. Ooh, he was a strange man. He'd be good to you, and then he didn't care what happened nowhere. He was buried on my birthday. That woman will have to look at me on the last day— the last hour. Ovie just throwed his life away, and she caught him asleep and killed him. But what did he go off with that thing for? He left us to live or die. But every dog has its day. I worked and killed myself to keep him from throwing his children away. I went barefooted, and just wore any old thing. I went through the cold weather, snow and ice, packing loads at midnight. But one day I'll rise and shine, for I ain't done nothing against nobody.

THE DREAM OF OVIE

I dreamed of Ovie one time. I thought he had a pale blue shirt on with his sleeves rolled up. And I thought me and him was on the porch a-skating, and we was having more fun. I thought ice was on the floor of the porch. Ovie would swing me around, and I'd swing him back. We was just having the best time. I dreamed of Ovie, and that was the night that Garson Smith was killed in Jones Creek. That Jones boy killed Garson Smith. And I dreamed of me and Ovie a-skating on the porch on ice. I thought me and him both started to go in the house, and we was going right through the door, side to side. We was kindly scrunched, and I sort of stepped in front of him, and I went on in. And then when I got inside, I looked back to see if he was coming with me. He wasn't there. And out of the bed I come.

JUST HERE A SHORT WHILE

They'll be something work. They'll be something to take care of me. Yeah. They will be. And if they don't, God has got a place for me to go on to.

I would help do anything for anybody that's got breath in them. Yeah man. I don't want to harm nothing. We're just here a short while, a few days, and full of trouble. But thank God we can live good, and it's a happy world—if we won't partake of the wrong things, why it's a happy world to be in.

BACK ON MAE'S PORCH

YOU'VE GOT A CONSCIENCE

It's a wonderful world to live in if people would just get the right thing and stand up on that and not let nothing lead them astray. And anybody, about anybody, knows right and wrong. You've got a conscience, and God will move on you when you are wrong. They's something that will tell you to not, and then something else maybe will say yes, go on and do it. Now you've got a conscience. I'm awful bad to mind my conscience. When anything says get up and take somebody something, if it's a bill of money or anything, I just get what it showed me, and then I take it to them.

THE PRAYINGEST MAN

One time Joe Wilson was a-coming down that hill over there where the old road was. He was a-coming down the hill to the Kildav Bridge. And about the time he hit the end of the Kildav Bridge, there come a puff of wind, and it took his umbrella away. And Joe said, "Lord, get my parasol." Poor old Joe. Yeah. He just went a-praying. If there ever could be anybody in heaven, Joe is. And old Joe prayed all the time. I went down there, and he prayed at the table. I'm telling you what's the truth. That's the prayingest man that I ever heard in my life. And he died, and his old woman died just in a few days after he died. They never got Joe buried good until Tildy died.

I ain't been led to go down there much. I don't know why. I guess I'm missing him so much. You hate to go anywhere and miss anyone so bad.

I sort of live one day at a time. We can't hardly plan nothing. When we live through this day, and dark comes, if we live to get home, we don't know whether we'll ever see another day or not. And it's hard to plan, but I generally know what I might do.

Now if I live and get strong, I'm going to get up in the spring and plant my garden—plant me a few rows of taters. But now I can't plant a hill nor nothing without planting the whole thing.

When the moon shines and I can look out there through the garden, they'll just be a hill—like it's in a book—a picture in a book. I know that I've had the prettiest gardens on that piece of ground. It's been wonderful. The joy that I've got—and that's all I raise a garden for is to watch it grow and then to get to give my neighbors good things out of the garden.

I took Miss Johnson ten good ripe tomatoes. I took Oma fifty pounds of taters. And I've never sold but one bushel of beans in my life out of my garden. And I give that woman enough beans back to pay her for what she give me for the beans.

I was getting Rose a pair of shoes. She was in the band, and I was getting her a pair of them white shoes to wear in the band. And I didn't have no money right then, so I let that woman have a bushel of beans to get Rose some band shoes.

I wasn't much able to work this year, and it's rained all of the time. But I'm going to raise me some garden next year if I'm a-living, and if I ain't, why, I'll be over in the graveyard with Matt and Bett.

THE WASHING

Dr. Eubank, she tries. She tries to help me. And I love her, and she's done about everything she knows to do. Seems like they's just things that's hard to understand. I ain't sick no way but being dead old and worked to death. And you know I've raised ten children—sent them to school, took them to church, and washed their clothes.

Most of the time, I washed clothes on a washboard. Once Ovie went and bought me a new washing machine. I had it about a week, and I washed a time or two with it. And you know that he up and took that washing machine down to the Robert Furniture Company, down at Baxter, and sold it for just a few dollars. And he had given three hundred and some dollars for that washing machine, but he took it and left me. There I stood. I had to go back to the washboard.

I wash right on the washboard. And I've got a plunger, and I can put my clothes and my detergent in the water, run me some water, and let my clothes set in the sun. I get that plunger, and plunger them clothes. And honey, I can wash anything as good as it can be washed. And I like to hang my clothes out and let the sun dry them. Clothes smell so good and clean when you sun dry.

I washed for them boys. They'd be a line of overalls—Ovie's overalls, and Matt's, and Hubert's, Estle's, and Dennis's. And them children went to school all the time, and I had all the washing to do, and I was working for the Lewises too. I was having to cook till we'd have something to eat—beans and stuff, when we'd come home for supper.

When I was at the Lewises', I went dressed up like I was in a hospital—never was dirty. My clothes was clean. If we had company, Miss Lewis would go to the store and get me a brand-new white uniform. I had my hair fixed and done up, and I had on good shoes that they'd buy me when they'd go to Lexington. They'd get me these things and their children little old things. They was real good to me.

Junior Lewis never give me a short word all the time that I worked for him. I worked fifteen years, and Junior was like a younger brother to me. And if I needed more money or if anything went wrong that caused me to have to go to the courthouse or anything, honey, don't you think that I didn't have backing.

CHANGING IT AROUND

I had that picture a-setting close by me. I missed my family so bad when I was gone to Florida, but I got along and was satisfied good. I had a little desk and a chair, and I could go and write. Oh, I learned to write real good, right in Florida, writing back home. I kept a letter in the mail all the time to some of them.

Then one day Miss Lewis took a notion to change it all around. She took that little chair till I wouldn't have the chair. And I wouldn't have the little table nor nothing. And when she moved that chair and table, and all the little old things I had in my room, all the pictures I had sitting around there from home, well, it made me get lonesome just to go back home. Yeah. Oh, I stayed two months, and I'll swear I just walked the floor over my children. My children had talked me into going.

Well, I went with the Lewises, them people I worked with. I went with them to help them on their vacation in Florida. I stayed two months, and honey, I never hardly sat down off of my feet. I done the awfulest lot of rugged work down there—cooking and cleaning after all of them. Seemed like I got along good until Miss Lewis moved that little table and moved them things where I'd go sit after I'd get the dishes washed and everything done. After Miss Lewis moved things, I was left just a-standing around. Before that happened, I'd go down in a little basement part of the building, and I'd write letters, and read things, and have a little bit of peace, and I'd rest for a few minutes.

You don't hardly get to rest when you stay with people and do their work. You're about busy all the time.

THE BABY PARTY

Last night they was a-doing things down there at the shower, and they would put a string around a girl's waist to see who could come the closest to cutting it the right length to fit her. The pregnant girl—they'd measure her, and ever who could guess the right length of string to go around her would get a gift. And honey, I got the gift for a-measuring the string.

The prize was two little pitchers. You could put salt and pepper in them, and they were the prettiest things. Some of them said, "Mae knowed what she was a-doing." They know me pretty good. I can look at anything and know what it ought to be. I don't miss nothing generally. And if anything ain't sewed right, I can see it, honey. If it's a breadth of a hair err, it's wrong.

I wouldn't fool with playing them cards. I wouldn't fool with that. I just watched them. But I hit that girl's size right on the nailhead, honey. Yeah. That tickled them to death over me a-guessing.

It was Miss Johnson or somebody who said, "You needn't fool with her." Said, "She can know what's in anything just the minute her eye hits it."

THE WEEDEATER

Oh, I can sure pour it to it a-cutting weeds with a weedeater, honey. I can cut the weeds.

Your yard's pretty.

You know my brother John. I bought that weedeater off of him. And he said, "Why you'll never learn to start it." It wasn't ten minutes till I had it a-mowing and a-cutting weeds. He said, "Boys, what about Mae." Said, "Well, she never had her hands on a weedeater till right now. And she just started it right off and went to cutting grass."

Oh, Helen Smith always said that if her mother had a-done like I did she wouldn't have lost her mind. Said if she'd had flowers, and fooled with the flowers, and got out and talked to people, she would have been all right.

I think it helps when you have other life around and beauty around you.

I'm so happy. I've studied about it. I enjoy everything. When I get up in the morning, I'm so proud to see the daylight and look out on the hillside. And if anybody comes to talk to me, I ain't got a problem. I'm ready to talk to them. I'm just doing pretty good. I'm just way old, but I've got sense with it too.

Well, you can get the almanac, and you can go right by it, and do right what it tells you—plant by the almanac. And see, I've experienced it. I've done raised stuff, and I know that it works well.

Now if you're planting corn in brand-new ground that ain't been tended a big lot, why, the old moon is good to plant on. For that new ground that ain't been used, why, it grows your corn so high—right on up. The ear of the corn will be up over the top of your head.

I always say, the older the ground is, why I'll plant it on the part of the old and new moon, and then the sign's in the arms. And it shows the moon, quarter, and everything right in the almanac. I'd better give you an almanac to go by. You might want to farm some down at your house. I'll give it to you, and I'll get me another one some way or other. That'll keep you from having to be a-searching around. You'd have it right in your hand, and you can take it with you. I've done got it in my head.

I can look at the moon and the seven stars. When spring comes, the seven stars is right over yonder where the hill and the sky meet. You see as far as you can see, and when you can see the seven stars—that's called the Great Dipper. Was you ever teached that at school? Well, that now—that's the seven stars.

And when spring is a-coming, you'll see the seven stars right over there. And they will come plumb across, and when it gets summer, and the spring is gone, the seven stars is over here on this side right at the top of the mountain. I've watched them many a year.

This is the north side of the mountain. I'd like to live on the south side. It's a lot better for farming. But I've growed ever what I wanted to, even on this north side. Boy, I've had gardens. And I've had hogs that you couldn't imagine, down in that hog lot. I covered that hog lot with tin so that it wouldn't rot down. I knowed after I had that stroke that I couldn't fool with hogs no more.

AIN'T THE TIME TO BE BENT OVER

It's a wonder I ain't growed over, ain't it? It ain't the time.

Oh God, have mercy, God. But the Lord gave us a mind to go by. And when you hump yourself down, and droop over, and just go half bent, blessed God, you'd better straighten up.

They's a woman not nearly as old as I am, and there's a hump on her back, honey.

Boy, my daddy was straight. When he put his good clothes on and walked out, why, he was better looking than my brothers was. He was a handsome man. He was ninety-six years old when he died. And he could dress up, and he was prettier than e'ry boy he had. It's the truth. Oh, he was built so neat in his clothes, and his clothes fit him so good. He had the prettiest feet and shoes. He wasn't slouchy a bit, and him way old. When he'd dress up to go to Leslie County, he looked like a young man.

EVERYBODY DYING, ONE AFTER THE OTHER

But oh I worked. I come and helped lift Mammy, and we kept her down at Gussie's house as long as we could. I'd get so tired talking to her and everything, but she's gone. And blessed God, Mammy died, and then in six months, Pap died. And then at Christmas, Matt died, my boy, and then in February, my brother Lewis died.

They took Lewis to be checked at the doctor's down at Hyden, and blessed God, they just got Lewis's shirt unbuttoned to set something on his chest to see how sick he was, and he fell dead right in that doctor's hands in the hospital. And then the ninth day of June, Bett got killed, and her two children were nearly killed. That's five of our family dying just one right after the other.

LITTLE BREATHS IN OUR BODY

We're here and, well, they's people gets it in their mind that nothing will never come their way. And honey, we're just here today, and we don't know where we'll be before dark comes or where we might be tomorrow. We don't know. We really, none of us, ain't got nothing here but little breaths in our body. And it's just like a vapor of smoke, the Bible says, a vapor. That's just like a puff of smoke coming and then be gone.

NEED ONE ANOTHER

The Lord blessed me. Why, I never had no education, but he sure gave me a good normal brain. I can size anything up pretty well and know what will work and what won't. I ain't been to school on it, but then again I know a whole lot too.

You know, I'm so crazy about young people, and my heart goes out to them more than anything. But I love people to the bottom of my heart. It ain't no put-on thing. I'd help them any way I can. We're just here—everybody is—and we need one another, some way or other.

TWO LITTLE FLOWERS

I was coming up the hill, but everything's a miracle to me, for me to think over. I was coming up the hill packing a few groceries, and my hip was so sore that I couldn't hardly get up the hill. And I sat down on a rock to rest a few minutes to make it on to the house. Two little girls come along and just reached and got them groceries. One said, "Give them to me." Well, I said, "They might be too heavy for you."

And she said, "No, I can pack it." Well, she set the bag on her hip, and just first one of them packed it a piece and then the other one. They was just right out there.

Well, I said, "You-uns are just so pretty." I said, "I don't know what I was a-waiting on, but it was for you-uns to come by." I looked down there. Them two little girls looked like two flowers, I'm a-telling you.

Young people is a special thing to me. I love young people, little children, big children. And young people needs us more than anything, besides trying to lower them down. Anyone that knows, that's lived over things, ought to tell—ought to talk to people, and explain things to younger people. And they might pick something up that would be good for theirself. We are required that—to counsel our younger people, give them good counsel, and tell them if we know something good. Tell them about it.

I just about worked all of my time away. I had so much to do. I just thought of getting it done. But I've kept them children warm. I would keep the fire going all night, and I would get up and mind the fire. I ain't got nary one burned up, nor nary one give away, nor nary one starved to death, nor nary one ever froze to death. I walked with them and will anybody.

God has got the whole world in his hand. He's got everybody's life . . . like a spoonful of water laying in the palm of your hand. He's got the whole thing. And if it hadn't been for the mercy in the hand of God, you know that I couldn't have raised ten children with no money.

I've been hard to kill. It's the hand of the One that put me here that helps me.

WALKING IN THE LIGHT

I'm just what I am now, and I'm satisfied with it. It don't disagree with me. I'm proud of living so many years. I have laid a pattern in front of me, and my background is good. If I can make it a little while longer, why, everything will be all right after a while.

God might keep us here a long time. I'm so glad over everything that the Lord made on earth—the mountains and the trees, and the gardens and the rocks, and everything. I appreciate everything and every step I make on the ground. I thank God for having the ground to walk on.

Every day you live, you'll appreciate life more. If you can just walk down the road here and back, why, it'll be something big for you to think on. That's the way I am about it now.

Be content. The Bible says, "Be content with what you've got, and walk in the light as you see the light." And when you get into a spot that you think ain't good, get out of it.

EASTER DINNER

Hmm, well, I'm cooking Easter dinner for us for tomorrow.

Bless your heart. I'll swear to God.

It's going to be chicken and pinto beans, and potatoes, and cucumbers and onions, and possibly, some cornbread, and I've fixed a cake. I baked it, but it looks kind of funny.

Well, that ain't nothing. We don't care. We'll eat it. Why, we don't care. It'll eat just as good.

I baked it in a skillet because, well, there weren't any cake pans.

Well, that's just as good. That's a-getting it from scratch, and that's what's good.

Yeah.

Oh God.

MEET IN THE MIDDLE

Boy, I love to hear these birds.

Yeah. When they sung every morning when I was in Florida, it would nearly kill me. Those birds would sing just like the birds would sing when Pap would plow every morning. We'd start to the field, and he'd go to plowing. And he'd holler and go to pranking with us children. And he'd say, "Let's get with it, boys. Yeah. We're working." Honey, oh, we just set the hoes afire a-hoeing, me and my ole brother. One would get at this end of the field and the other one at the other end. And when Pap would get it plowed, why, we would meet each other in the middle. Buddy, when you hoed corn for my daddy, it was hoed good. Pap learned us how to hoe. Yeah. Oh God.

TALK TO THE CHILDREN

Ms. Phillips, you know you were talking about waking up
in the night?

Yeah.

This morning I had this—it was a nice thing, but it was
an unusual thing happening. Like before I got awake, I had this
sense of feeling like if I died that I'd be dipped back into God—like
my spirit would go back into God, and then I'd come out again still
being myself. It was an interesting feeling. For some reason, lately,
I've been thinking a lot about dying. I don't know why, but I think
it's because I'm appreciating life so much.

Well, I know what's got you to thinking over things. Now
your boy being gone to the Navy, you've got someone to pray
about as well as yourself. Pray that God keeps his hand over him
and that Jeff turns his heart to the Lord. Pray that if anything
was to go wrong that he would go right. Lord, I tried to teach
my children good and get them to do right. But grown people
just does about the way they want to. But you know we're
required to talk to our children, and to pray for them, and
try to help them up through life.

STAND BEFORE GOD
AND NOT BE ASHAMED

My sister is crippled over. I packed her to the store and her a great big child. We went to the store, and it went to raining. I bought Mammy a new dishpan and turned it over my sister's head to shelter her from the rain a-hitting her. I thought that it wouldn't do for a drop of rain to touch her. I thought that she was so precious. I've always thought my family was. But I love everybody. If I had to die right now, I don't care how lowdown they are, or where they're from, there's some reason for them being here, and God knows why.

But I'm a-going somewhere someday, and I won't be back. And I want to stand before God and not be ashamed of myself, if I can. If I know what to do, I want to strive for that. I do. They'll be so many people there I'll be looking for.

Now I've just been like I am—natured like I am. I've had a good heart for people, but I've got a temper. If anyone comes at me in the wrong way, why, I can be sort of got off my rocker, but it ain't hard for me to get back on. I won't put nothing on nobody that I don't want to take myself. I want to treat people like I want to be treated and live that way, and I have. I've been good to people. They's been no one to come in the background to say nothing that I've done to them. I don't owe nobody nothing, not nothing.

I feel so good. You know I walked upright before man and God. I married my children's daddy that's in the grave. He left us and caused himself to be killed. And I just worked on. I've got my young-uns, got his young-uns, and I worked and raised them, sent them to school, took them to church, and buried him good, and put the headstone to his grave. And I've just lived on. Let the world roll on. I never had time to look back to see if there was e'ry man on the side nor nothing. I didn't have time, not when you've got about ten children to take care of—and Ovie left us right when we needed him. I didn't have a car nor no way to get around. I walked on my feet to work to keep them children fed. But God is a great God, and he's a big thing.

Nothing never bothered me. I walked in the black dark a-coming home from work. I'd be afraid now to go from here over on that mountain where I worked, on account of maybe being killed right on the road. But I used to come in the black dark, and I'd pray to God for nothing to bother me, for me not to see nothing that I'd be afraid of. I never see'd as much as a dog in the road. I never see'd nothing that would interfere with me a bit.

But Lord, I've give my life for my children. But I'd whup them if they was fifty-nine years old or seventy. They'd better mind their Mammy.

A WATER BUCKET

Hubert's wife, she'll walk right by him. She'll go with him. She won't leave him, nor forsake him, don't seem like. I hope it holds good.

When you've got a water bucket and buy it, it won't leak then, but if you ain't careful and don't take good care of it, it'll go to leaking. And trouble could come in on some corner you wouldn't think about.

LINING UP THE FENCE POSTS

If you can't see where you're wading in the river, you better not go in. You might get in to where you couldn't get out. I want to know what I'm a-doing. Now we have to line up. We have to line ourselves up right.

I leaned fence posts right till I could stand to look at them. My daddy would always step back and side over to see if they was lined up right.

If a person would take interest in something that's good instead of bad, it'd be for the better. What about when I was little—I learned myself to not fool with anything that wasn't good. I wouldn't fool with it at all. If it was good, like sewing, or anything real important, I was right in on learning about that.

You know I never had no books at school. People back then couldn't get books for their children. And me and a little neighbor boy would sit together, and I studied in his books with him. I went and graduated through the sixth grade.

CLOSE TEACHING PARENTS

You know a lot of people takes the wrong side of everything, but I never did, but I had close teaching parents over me. My daddy and mother was awfully careful with their children. One time my daddy hit me one little lick with a switch. He was mad at Shel. Shel had done some big thing, and Daddy was real mad. When Pap would have to whup him e'ry a lick, it'd nearly kill Pap. He didn't want to whup Shel, and when he whupped Shel, well, that made Pap mad, and then Pap sort of whupped me. Mammy got all over him, and she told him to never do that again in his life. Said, "Don't you lay a finger on her when she ain't done a thing to be whupped for." Said, "Don't do it again now."

Pap never done it no more, and he was talking about it right before he died. He said that was the only lick that he ever hit me in his life, yes sir, didn't have to. I minded my parents. Yeah. I thought what they said was what for me to do, and I done it. If it'd been wrong, I guess I'd done the same thing. But they teached me good.

EVERY BLESSING

I thank the Lord for everything, every blessing of life, and for my good neighbors and good friends that comes to see me. It's good to be good, and live good—have a good heart toward people, for God will make a way. He'll take good care of us. He'll supply our needs. We have to work, and go and get it, but he'll make us able, or he'll make us be till we couldn't.

It's a wonderful thing for people to enjoy their life all they can, and just work, and move right on, and do what they need to do. I've had a good country mountain living. My family, and the way we worked, it's all been a pleasure. It pleases me to death to talk over it. And some people say, "Do you just purely love to work?" But you know I do. It don't hurt me. When something's a-getting done, when we're in the garden and are hoeing, and a-cleaning the weeds out, and the garden's beautiful and growing, it's a pleasure. People ought to let their mind run on stuff like that.

LET ENOUGH BE ENOUGH

Now what's the matter with the world today is people's minds are drifting off, and people are doing something mean or stealing something off of somebody or are making trouble to somebody instead of getting down and working, making and having pretty things a-growing, or flowers around in the yard to work with. They's something to do besides being mean. And anyone could find things. It's a pleasure to get to walk around with nothing to worry about. One can get food and not be sick.

Why, there's people who can't be content for nothing. And you know the Bible says to be content with what you've got, even if it's just a little bit. Be content with it. Let enough be enough.

FREE FROM YOUR HEART

I have give and shared with anybody that has ever come
about me, and I'll give them pop or give them anything that I've
got that they want to eat. Or if I can help them in any way, I'll
do it. Anything a-being free from your heart, that's what counts.

Well, they's people thinks that something a-being brand-new
is what matters. You know, Phyllis, I'd rather just live what I've
lived. If we had everything on earth, you know we'll just die and
go on anyhow. Now I don't know why, but I ain't never had much
of nothing. Why, we've got by good, but as to having beautiful
things a-setting out there and things just to show off, I ain't had
nothing. But lah, I've had beautiful gardens, and I've had pretty
flowers, and I've had my own stock—had the cattle. Neighbors
would take care of them. I had my children, had good food to eat,
and had good clothes on. But they's people that's got everything
it looks like that a heart could wish for, and they ain't satisfied
with nothing. They're killing theirself and killing their young-uns.
And Lord, we have to be content, and share with others, and have
a heart for others. Yes.

SOMETHING GROWING
INSIDE OF YOU

And that builds the building, honey. It's having something growing inside of you that God will approve of, is the important thing. Yes sir. And no beauties of this world ain't going to take us nowhere. But I thank God for everything I've had. It was just for me to know how to put things together that he puts here, and make something out of it.

And I can live with money or without money. I can just about fix anything that I need fixed. I can about work on anything and make something out of nothing.

I believe if I had everything in the world that it wouldn't be no more to me than just what I've already got. Nothing don't move me up, nor it don't blow me up. It was just for me to live like I live. It's a parable. And it's exciting to think over how I've managed and done to raise ten children and not have no man to help.

I'm doing pretty good. But if anything gets the matter now, I could jump off the porch and run to the top of the hill. I've got nerve like a mule—pure mule. Pap had some mules natured just like me.

We're just here, and we're going somewhere later. The Bible says, "Love our neighbor like ourselves." Now that's a commandment, and I sure live it.

PRECIOUS GOOD PEOPLE

Anyone's people, neighbors, and good friends is all they got in this life. Ain't it? Well, that's all I got. I ain't got no big living nor nothing, but Lord, what precious good people I got.

A ROAD TO TRAVEL

Well, we have to live through our young days, and as we live up, let our mind keep lined out on the right side. They's a left and a right, and I believe that anyone is supposed to try to keep theirself on the right side of everything, on account of we've got a road to travel, and God knows everything, and he sure will take care of us.

My parents taught if we went to anybody's house to not walk right on in. My daddy told us to call at the gate, and see if anybody would answer the door and ask us in, to come on in. We was raised really careful and good. We was raised to work, and we had to manage everything to make money and survive. We cut wood on the mountain to make fire. We sawed with a crosscut saw. I can saw like a man right now. I can help. I can saw as good as anybody that ever took hold of a saw, for I know exactly the way it has to be swung for it to cut. My daddy said he'd rather saw with me than e'ry man in Leslie County.

Why, it's a wonder this arm ain't worn off and gone. If you could see the logs, the saw logs, that I helped my daddy cut with a crosscut saw. But I have been strong, honey. I've been strong. It'll be hard for me to get plumb old and get down.

That's good. I'm glad that it's going to be hard, so you won't get down. I love you, Ms. Phillips.

I love you too, honey.

AFTERWORD

After living close to Mae for a year and a half and recording her stories, I went to Tucson, Arizona, to attend graduate school for cultural studies. I lived in Tucson for three years. During the summers I would visit Mae. After receiving my M.A. in comparative cultural and literary studies, I returned home to Kentucky, and I visited Mae. She was now bedridden and faded in and out of reality. I sat by her bedside and held her hand. I was so happy to see her, but I was saddened by her condition.

I said, "Ms. Phillips, I am so glad to see you."

Mae said, "I want to tell you a story."

Mae was not looking at me. She was looking straight ahead. She said, "There once was a girl, a young woman, who came over here, and she looked like she just came from around the corner. Yeah, and she looked like she was in need of loving. And oh, how I loved her. And she loved me. We had the best of times. But it broke my heart when she went away. She said she had to go west to go back to school. I missed her so much when she went away. It plumb broke my heart."

I was squeezing Mae's hand, and I could feel tears rolling down my cheeks. I felt a deep burning as I learned how my leaving had hurt Mae. I struggled to say, "Mae, it's me. It's me, Phyllis. I'm back. I'm back home now. I'm here. It's me, Phyllis."

Mae looked toward me. She said, "Phyllis, is that you?"

I said, "Yes. It's me. I'm back."

Mae said, "Phyllis, well, I swear to God. It's you."

I said, "Yes, and I love you so much, and I am so very glad to see you."

Mae said, "Well, Lord, I'm glad to see you too."

Mae Phillips died peacefully on August 20, 2006. Before she died I read her stories back to her, and at the end of my reading she smiled and said, "Now that's a good book."

THANK YOU

Jerry Johnson, for introducing me to Ms. Phillips, for your great insight, and for your invaluable help with this project.

Gurney Norman, my friend, for being a voice of wisdom and a steadfast guide from the beginning.

Henry Wallace, for your belief in me, for your belief in the importance of this project, and for your friendship.

Martha Whitaker, my dear friend, for your enthusiastic support of the telling of Mae's story.

Scott Momaday, for your recognition of the value of Mae's story, and for your words of encouragement.

Ibrahim Imam, for your friendship, and for your dedication in providing skillful technical support.

Tom Hardin, for your great suggestions about the choice of photographs for this book.

Tom Moran and Laura Faber, for providing darkroom equipment so that I could print the photographs for this book.

Anne Bornschein, Rita Cron, Carl Helmich, and Judy Steer for your expertise in proofreading and editing.

Nelda Wyatt, for your reliable friendship.

Bill Owens, for valuing this project enough to play a significant role in bringing Mae's story to fruition.

Barbara Hancock, for your insightful comments, for your generous support, and for your friendship.

Julius Friedman and Carol Johnson, for applying your great talent and intelligence to the design of this book. Working with you was a true delight.

Ken Eberhart, for your good counsel. Thank you for skillfully guiding me—with great care and understanding—through the publishing process.

Jeffrey Scott, my son, my greatest thanks go to you. Like Mae, you are courageous, creative, and compassionate.